S0-AID-197

Welcome

ENTER ANOTHER PLACE

AND TIME — A VIRTUAL

VILLAGE FULL OF SHOPS

ALL DEDICATED TO

THE POSSIBILITIES OF

USING FABRIC IN YOUR

SCRAPBOOKS. AS THE

BELL ON EACH SHOP

DOOR SIGNALS YOUR

ENTRANCE, YOU'LL BE

SURROUNDED BY IDEAS

BOTH CHALLENGING AND

SIMPLE. SOME PROJECTS

REQUIRE A BIT OF SEWING,

OTHERS JUST A GLUE

STICK; BUT ALL OF THEM

WILL WEAVE A SPELL

OF INSPIRATION FOR

PROJECTS YET TO COME.

TABLE OF *Contents*

PAGE 4

1

PAPERIE

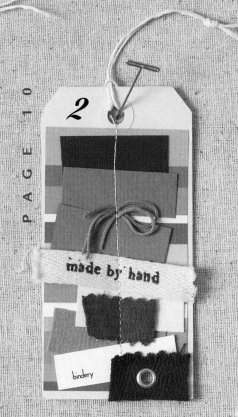

PAGE 10

2

made by hand

bindery

PAGE 14

3

boutique

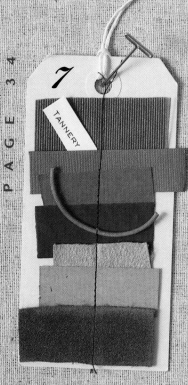

PAGE 34

7

TANNERY

PAGE 38

8

tailor

PAGE 42

9

527

Rice Paper

Spinnaker

PAGE 18   4   lingerie

PAGE 22   5   Ooh La La   seamstress

PAGE 26   6   It's a Girl   nursery baby   nursery kids

PAGE 48   10   Hand Woven   pharmacy

PAGE 56   11   GALLERY

PAGE 60   12   Center back Place on fold   haberdashery

CHAPTER 1

Steal a peek inside the window of a Paperie and you'll find it's very similar to your favorite fabric store: explosions of color, lush textures and brand new designs. Our artists have juxtaposed the two mediums, making it difficult to tell where the paper ends and the fabric begins. You'll have to decide if Ruth's photo mats are paper or fabric or if Tena's *Lexi* layout uses papier-mâché or a cutting-edge fabric-mâché technique. Look closely and discover how versatile fabric can be when combined with paper, then take a turn at composing your own mixed-media masterpiece.

THE BRIDE'S CLOSET BY DEBBIE

Cover a hanger with three pages from a wedding etiquette book. Tack the pages on with buttons, hand stitches, ribbon and a daub of glue. Print the shower details onto fabric, cut into a tag shape and set an eyelet at the top. Insert a walnut-inked tag in the pocket (created by the overlapping papers) for the guests to write advice, a quote or a memory.

THE WEDDING GIFT BOX
BY DEBBIE

Line a box with fabric. Package wedding memorabilia in labeled glassine envelopes or tins or tie with twill and ribbon. Accent tags with flowers from fabric. Stitch closely around the flower and trim off excess fabric.

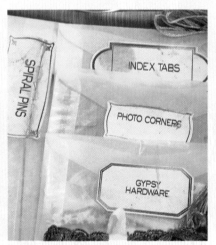

BRIGHT EYES
BY RUTH

Sew paper or fabric over photographs by stitching just inside the edge. Stitch again 1/2" in from the original stitching, then cut out the very center, pinking the edges. Set eyelets along the edges of all pieces and connect with ribbon.

ALYSSA NICOLE
BY TENA

Draw a design onto cardstock, then glue thin twine to the design. When completely dry, adhere another piece of cardstock on top and gently emboss with a popsicle stick. Machine stitch on both sides of the embossing.

VARIATIONS:
Use thicker twine, sew on only one side of the embossing or darken the embossed area with chalk.

LEXI
BY TENA

Cut nine 2" wide strips of fabric and tie a knot in the end of each. Sew strips together side by side. Saturate fabric with fabric stiffener, then twist and wring out. Allow to dry on plastic. Dip ribbon in stiffener and form the title. Put a plastic bag on top of a mouse pad and use straight pins to hold the word in position until dry.

FEMININE
BY JULIE T.

Accordion fold and crease (with an iron) a piece of silk organza and place over patterned paper. Back a piece of satin with patterned paper. Make small slits in the fabric and fold back to reveal the paper. Tack the fold with a pearl bead and ribbon. For the bottom, print scanned paper and a definition onto sheer organza.

LOVE MANY THINGS
BY RENEE

Machine stitch fabric and ribbon around a photo. Machine stitch only the top of the top-left swatch, allowing the fabric to be lifted to reveal journaling. Stamp title onto fabric, and accent with ribbon and brads.

FABRIC DOLL JOURNALS
BY DONNA

Fold 8 1/2" x 6" cardstock in half. Create a doll on the front using fabric and machine stitches. Fold three lengths of cardstock just smaller than the cover to make the inside pages. Staple spine to bind.

MIRACLE
BY JANELLE

Cover foam board with paper and batting. Sew buttons through all layers for a quilted look. Cut letter and envelope from dyed twill. Hinge the envelope to the layout to reveal another photo and a quotation. Stamp and write the quote onto fabric by first prepping the surface with paint and a decoupage medium.

GRANDMA'S JOURNAL
BY CAROL

Scan and print fabric onto text weight paper and use it to cover the main part of the book. Cover the hinged portion with fabric overlapping onto the main cover for added strength. Bind with fabric-covered buttons and waxed linen.

Bindery

Check out what's hip and fresh at the Bindery: fabric hinges, printing on fabric and book cloth sliding from the spine to the title. Fabric can jazz up any binding or book cover, making a distinctive project that's bound to impress.

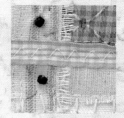

HEART AND SOUL BY CAROL

Embellish seven panels of canvas with image transfers, ribbon, trim, fabric, beads, etc. Bind into an accordion book with fabric hinges.

MATERIALLY SPEAKING BY DEBBIE

Scan fabric and print on textured paper. Fold into cards. Add a sentiment printed on fabric. To make the cover, fold cardboard in half. Cut floral fabric to just larger than the cardboard. Cut a piece of linen for the inside and fold up bottom edge to create a pocket. Affix fabric to cardboard with a glue stick, then stitch around the outside. Close with a button and twill.

PUPPY LOVE BY CAROL

Print scanned paper onto fabric. Pillow sew covers with batting inside. Weave ribbon through buttonholes made on the cover. Pull ribbon in rows one, three and five to the back cover. Stitch the ribbon in place at the outside edges. Insert small pieces of ribbon through the spine edge and tie along the outside.

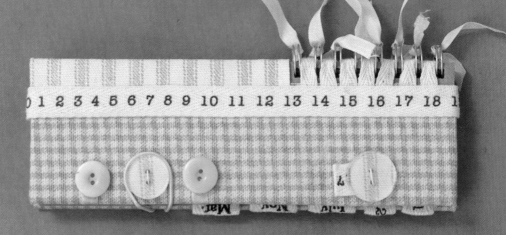

SKETCH JOURNAL
BY DONNA

Create your own bookcloth using directions on page 68. Use printed twill to create fabric tabs for each section.

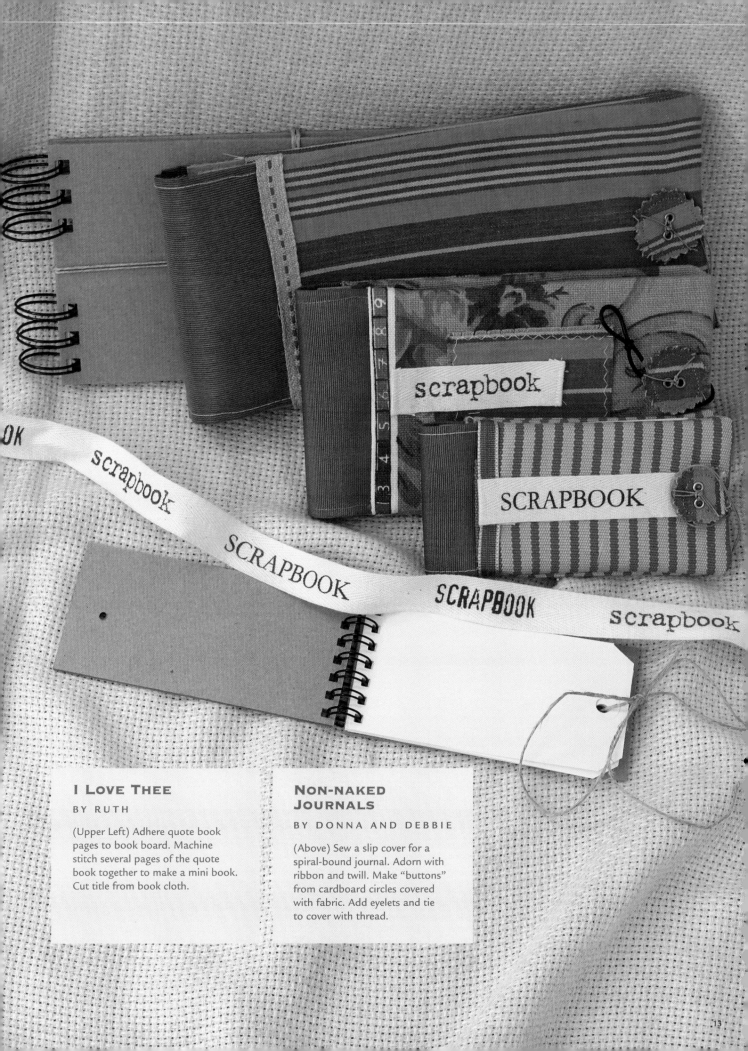

I Love Thee

BY RUTH

(Upper Left) Adhere quote book pages to book board. Machine stitch several pages of the quote book together to make a mini book. Cut title from book cloth.

Non-naked Journals

BY DONNA AND DEBBIE

(Above) Sew a slip cover for a spiral-bound journal. Adorn with ribbon and twill. Make "buttons" from cardboard circles covered with fabric. Add eyelets and tie to cover with thread.

SILK FABRIC JOURNAL
BY JULIE V.

Iron fusible web to silk fabric. Create a patchwork with the fabric and cut into squares and rectangles. Add decorative machine stitches. Construct title using various letter types. Enclose in a vinyl pocket and stitch to the cover. Cover chipboard with embellished fabric to make a front and back cover. Stitch the covers to a fabric spine and stitch signatures to the spine. Tie off threads to the outside.
(Right - Inside view)

Boutique

There's nothing like a trip to a funky Boutique where ultra-hip ideas make your imagination run wild. Ever thought of making a mini book out of designer fabric swatches or giving a new twist to old costume jewelry by sticking some on your page? You'll end up with more flair and style than you ever thought possible. So grab your girlfriends and invest in some quality retail therapy— the inspiration is free!

CORSET BOOK BY CAROL

Remove the insides of two same-sized books. Cut the covers so they create a book with a gated cover. Cover the book with velvet using satin trim and ribbon to create a laced-up "corset" look.

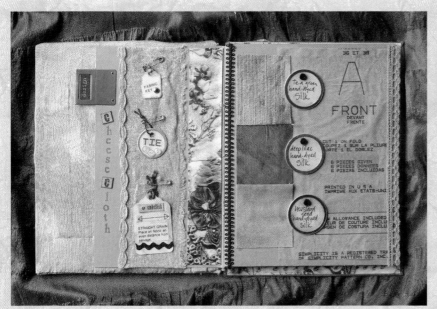

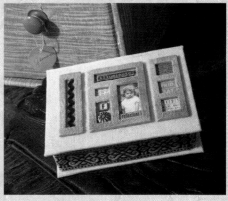

FABRIC GIFT BOX
BY JULIE V.

Construct a box from chipboard. Cover the bottom and top flap with a layer of calico and book-binder's mull. Wrap outer box with embroidered ribbon. Decorate the top with embellished silk frames.

15

HANA MY GEM
BY RUTH

Adhere fusible interfacing to wrong side of fabric. Cut fabric into wavy strips. Cut strips by layering each successive strip over the previous one and cutting them together so they match and make two 12" squares of fabric. Weave the pieces together to make one 12" x 12" page. Iron onto cardstock to secure.

HORTON PLAZA
BY TENA

Brush green paint on distressed corrugated cardboard. Cut fabric swatches in varying lengths so the different fabrics cascade down the page. Attach fabrics to the background with grommets and bead chain. Add fabric labels and a title printed on a transparency.

San Diego, California

Horton Plaza
Shopping expedition

Sights

Stores

Food

THE WORLD IS YOUR CANVAS
BY TRACY

Iron interfacing to the wrong side of fabric. Cut three sizes of flowers from fabric so they can be layered. Stitch flowers together and add a circle for the center. Affix ribbon at the top and bottom of photo.

THE WORLD IS YOUR CANVAS
2 pAint

JULY 2004

JOYFUL SOUL
BY LESLIE

Stitch ribbon and strips of fabric and paper to background. Stitch journaling blocks to page. Embellish matted photo with painted canvas and metal strips.

Here I am - 32 years old and the happiest I've ever been. Not only is my soul at peace... it is full of joy and appreciation for the life I've been given. It is not a perfect life... but a perfectly wonderful life just the same.

*blessed with 2 beautiful children
*lucky to have a husband I also call my bestest of best friends
*enjoying a hobby that nurtures me
*surrounded by a close-knit family and parents that love me always
*proud of who I am
*complete, full, happy and smiling

J O Y F U L

soul (sol), n. the spiritual part of a human being a person. -soul-ful a., expressing an elevated feeling soul-less a., mean, prosaic. (O.E. sawol)

I part of -soul-ful feeling -

Lingerie

Experience the feminine feel that dreamy fabrics can add to your work. Tuck photos or treasures behind strips of sheer ribbon for an innocent, romantic look or venture out and experiment with the possibilities of lingerie fasteners, such as hooks, snaps and garters. Whether the subject is a blushing bride or a bashful ballerina, a visit to the Lingerie shop is guaranteed to provide unmentionable inspiration.

EMALI'S TURN BY DEBBIE

(Above) Obtain fabric, lace and trim from the bride's close relatives' wedding dresses or veils. Label and position each piece around the bride's photo in a glass frame.

EM'S A BRIDE BY DONNA

(Right) Stitch silk ribbon to make a border and to divide page into thirds. Stitch sheer fabric to paper, forming pockets. Cut a heart shape from cardstock and cover with buttons and beads.

FOR ME? BY DEBBIE

(Far Right) Dip cheesecloth in a Kool-Aid mixture or color washes. Wring out, blot on a paper towel and allow to dry. To form the petals, cut four 3" squares of dyed cheesecloth. Alternating points of the square, lay the squares on top of each other, then fold all four in half together. Tightly roll a third of the way across and loosely wrap the rest around the roll. Fashion the leaves out of another folded square of gauze. Stitch across the bottom to secure. Print message on ribbon.

GROW

ALL DOLLED UP
BY RENEE

Surround a matted photo with ribbon and fabric. Attach journaling and title strips under sheer fabric and ribbon. Sew around each piece and around the entire layout, securing any loose materials.

ALL DOLLED UP

YOU LOOKED SO BEAUTIFUL THIS EASTER MORNING.

YOU WERE ANGELIC WITH YOUR WHITE DRESS, CURLED HAIR, AND PRECIOUS SMILE.

EASTER 2004
APRIL

Attire says...
"I am young and innocent."
Headband says...
"I am loveable and sweet."
Messy hair says...
"I am just a playful little girl."
Expression says...
"Don't mess with me... I'm feisty."

Put it all together and you get...

SASSY Audrey.

06.13.04 - Mum's birthday during a volleyball game - thus the messy hair.

SASSY AUDREY BY JENNIFER

Print journaling on patterned paper and add enlarged photo as shown. Cut flower from satin fabric. Cut various sizes of circles from sheer fabric and machine stitch on top of flower. Secure pink sheer material with mesh eyelets. Tie knots in a strip of material for the stem. Rubber stamp name on fabric and stitch in place.

For the left page, cover white cardstock with sheer pink fabric, letting the selvage edge hang over the side. Add sheer fabric over the title. Gather a strip of tulle and attach to the bottom. For the right page, print text onto organdy and attach over photos with ribbon. Add sheer fabric over journaling at the bottom.

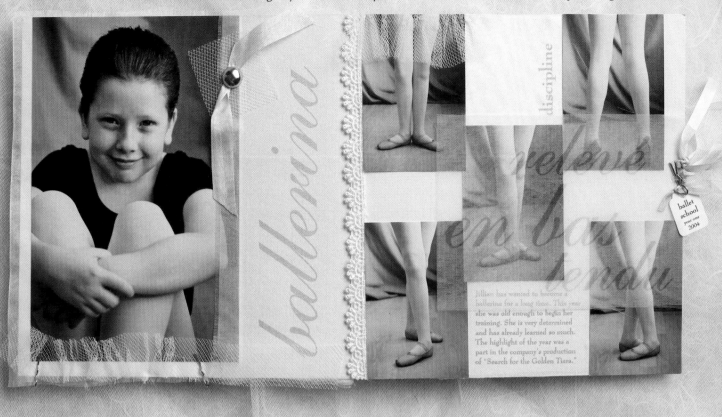

GRANDMA'S TRUNK

BY RUTH

Layer assorted papers on background. Collage antique findings and ephemera around photo.

Seamstress

Who's most familiar with fabric, decorative stitching and what's in vogue in the world of sewing? A seamstress, of course! In her store, you're in for a tactile experience as you handle the beautifully embroidered dishtowels, the masterfully smocked dress or the carefully constructed crazy quilt. Inspired by these techniques, our artists have sewn up their layouts, wall hangings and book covers. Tune up your sewing machine and add a stitch or two to your own work.

SHOE BY TRACY

Attach strips of fabric and ribbon to white cardstock. Add decorative stitches between fabric and ribbons. Cut at a diagonal and attach to background. Tie ribbon around a strip of paper and stitch on snaps for accents.

SWEET SAMANTHA BY TENA

Create a tri-fold layout, and crazy quilt the two outer flaps. Embellish the seams with decorative machine stitches using rayon and metallic threads. Add fibers to the surface with a couching stitch.

23

TEA
BY MIRIAM

Fold linen napkin so all points meet in the center, creating four pockets. Print journaling onto muslin, then stitch to a tag. Sew two coasters together and embellish with journaling. Mount main photo on foam board and stitch on twill letters with French knots.

TRAITS
BY RENEE

Quilt all fabric pieces and journaling together. Attach to cardstock base, machine stitching around entire layout to secure. Use iron-on letters for the title and secure appliqué flowers with adhesive dots.

WE CAN NOT DECIDE WHO YOU ARE MOST LIKE. SOMETIMES YOU ARE LIKE YOUR DADDY WITH HIS EXPRESSIONS: LIKE CUTTING YOUR EYES, ALWAYS HAMMING IT UP FOR THE CAMERA, BEING NOSEY, CURIOUS, AND OBSERVANT, AND STRIVING TO MAKE OTHERS LAUGH. YOU HAVE GOT YOUR DADDY'S UNI-BROW, THE BATSON ROUND FACE, AND NAILS, AS WELL AS HIS HAIRLINE. SOMETIMES YOU ARE LIKE YOUR MOMMY: MAKING THE MOST DRAMATIC EXPRESSIONS AND SOUNDS, ALWAYS SINGING AND DANCING, AND WRINKLING UP YOUR NOSE WHEN YOU LAUGH. YOU HAVE ALMOST THE SAME PROFILE AND FROM YOUR NOSE TO YOUR TOP LIP IT IS UNCANNY HOW CLOSELY YOU RESEMBLE HER. YOU HAVE GOT YOUR MOMMY'S COLOR OF HAIR. ~ YOU ARE PROBABLY MORE PHYSICALLY LIKE THE NEELY SIDE OF THE FAMILY. YOU HAVE A LOT OF BATSON CHARACTERISTICS, BUT AS FAR AS APPEARANCES THERE ARE TONS OF RESEMBLANCES TO THE NEELY FAMILY TREE. SO LET'S JUST SAY YOU ARE A PERFECT MIXTURE OF US ALL!

LEANNA RACHEL
2 1/2 YEAR PORTRAITS

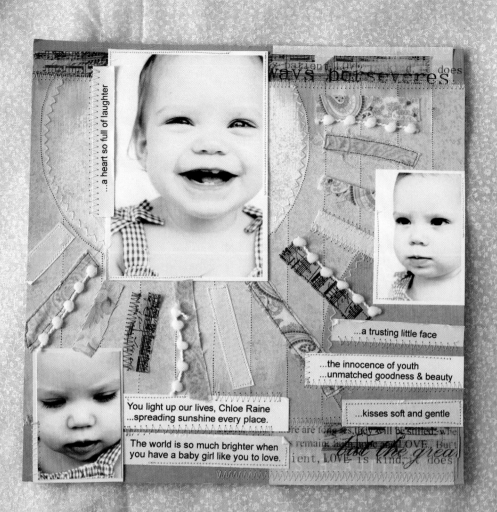

a heart so full of laughter

...a trusting little face

...the innocence of youth
...unmatched goodness & beauty

You light up our lives, Chloe Raine
...spreading sunshine every place.

...kisses soft and gentle

The world is so much brighter when
you have a baby girl like you to love.

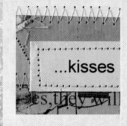

...kisses

SUNSHINE
BY LESLIE

Draw lines on paper,
then run through
sewing machine
without thread.
Spray with walnut
ink, allow to dry
and mount on dark
cardstock. Stitch
on tissue paper and
transparency strips
that have been
painted green.
Rub acrylic paint
across background.
Adhere or machine
stitch fabric strips
to make sun rays.

Made with love
and kisses

Ooh La La

unquestionably you
mikenna's book of endless questions

UNQUESTIONABLY
YOU
BY RUTH

Smock taffeta to the
front of the book.
Stitch signatures to
book with ribbon,
and use ribbon to
sew decorative stitches
along the edge of
each page.

Ooh La La

s real name?

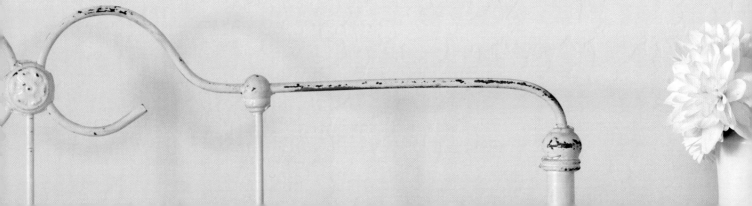

GRACIE'S DRESS
BY DONNA

Cover foam board with paper and use as the background in a pre-purchased ledge frame. Drill a hole at the top and attach a 7gypsies doorknob. Form a hanger from heavy wire and use to hang a dress and photo. Embroider a name on fabric for the title.

CHAPTER 6

Cozy into a rocking chair and turn on the classical music; a stroll through the Nursery will have you singing lullabies. Our artists will lull you with their ideas to bring nostalgia to your projects. Janelle preserves her newborn's onesie by adding it right on her layout and Miriam hides tender thoughts in itty-bitty pockets. Talk quietly as you "ooh" and "ahh" over this symphony of sweet ideas to showcase baby photos and memories.

THUMBS UP
BY MIRIAM

Make three small pillows from a dishtowel. Stuff one with batting and leave the other two open like a pillowcase. Print journaling on fabric, roll up and place inside. Rubber stamp the first letters of each word using a mixture of white gesso and masking fluid as the ink. Let dry, then paint the title background with watercolors. Embroider the rest of the title. Tie painted clear buttons with waxed linen.

CURTAIN CALL
BY DEBBIE

Hand stitch nine hankies together at the corners and halfway in between. Stitch one clip in each square and clip curtain to rings. Tie ribbon to inside corners. Slip curtain on a rod and attach photos.

LAYETTE
BY RUTH

Make a loom using foam core and pins. Place the pins along the top and bottom edges 1/2" apart. Measure photo onto loom and place pins along the top and bottom of where the photo will go. String embroidery floss from top to bottom so it goes over each pin. Leave a hole for the photo. Weave background using chenille and torn cotton fabric.

Iron a photo onto booties. Attach clear buttons that have been backed with fabric. Use t-shirt transfer paper to transfer photo to white muslin. Stitch to burp cloth. Add chenille rickrack and a clear button backed with fabric. Embellish a cap with chenille rickrack and clear buttons backed with fabric.

To make the quilt, iron photos and journaling onto quilt squares. Sew the squares wrong sides together. Clip edges to the seam. Bind quilt by stitching around outside edge and clipping to the seam. Wash and tumble dry low to rough up the edges.

BABY OZZIE
BY JANELLE

Cover foam board with fabric. Replace the onesie tag with a custom tag, then tack the onesie in place. Cover a shipping tag with fabric and photos. Cut swatches from items used at the hospital. Print main photo onto inkjet fabric, then "upholster" it to the page by stuffing with batting then setting with upholstery tacks. For the title, print letters onto fabric, then cover buttons with the fabric. Attach letters to ribbon.

CUTER
BY TRACY

Cut circles from fabric and attach to cardstock for stability. Stitch a spiral on each circle. Stitch photo to background and attach circles, using foam squares under some for dimension.

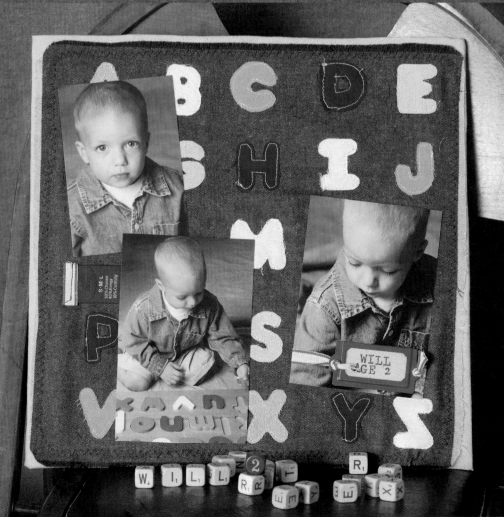

WILL AGE 2
BY TENA

Cut letters from fabric and lightly adhere them to denim. Stitch to secure. Zigzag stitch the embellished denim to another piece of fabric, then stretch it around a piece of chipboard for support.

Print a photo onto canvas. Stitch pieces of fabric and patterned
paper around photo. Cut initial from fabric and stitch in place. Print
journaling onto a negative transparency. Overlap with belt loops

funny   loyal

brave

happy

cool

fun

...we are so
proud of all
that you are!

POCKET BOOK

BY CAROL

Fill pockets from children's clothes with found objects. Add to journal pages which have been painted or covered with cloth or paper.

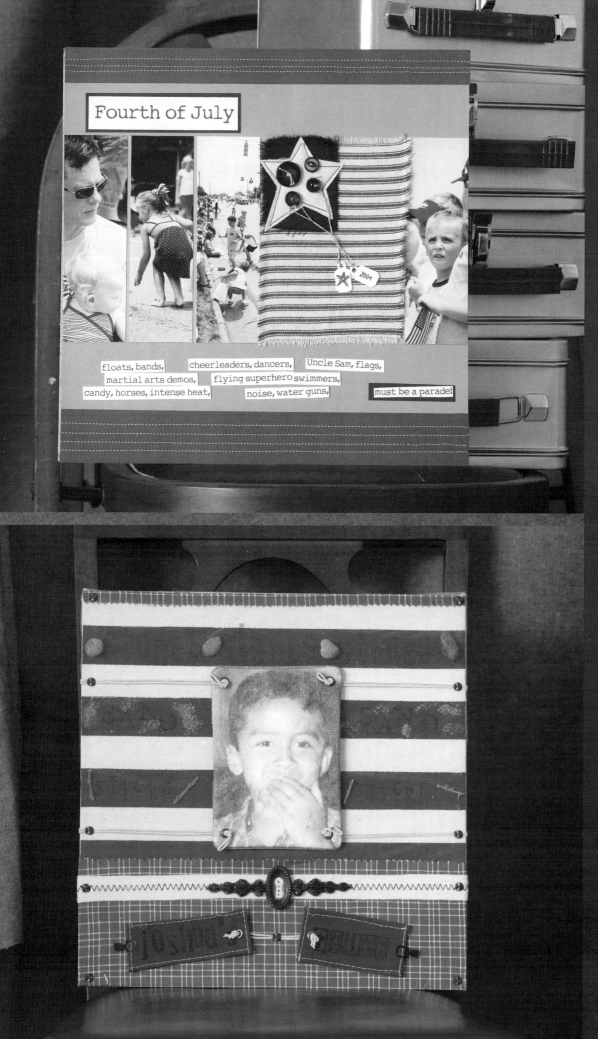

Fourth of July

floats, bands, cheerleaders, dancers, Uncle Sam, flags, martial arts demos, flying superhero swimmers, candy, horses, intense heat, noise, water guns, must be a parade!

FOURTH OF JULY

BY CATHY

Fashion a flag from fabric and buttons. Add straight stitching at the top and bottom of layout to mimic the stripes within the ticking.

JOSHUA'S BEST STUFF

BY CAROL

Tape stripes with masking tape and brayer over exposed areas with texture paint. Allow to dry and remove masking tape. To create canvas labels, brush paint over canvas. When dry, stamp words with permanent ink and machine stitch around the outside. To keep sticks, stones and sand from falling off, lay tulle over the top and stitch in place.

Tannery

Rich, supple leather. Soft, smooth suede. Musky, masculine scents. You might be touring the Tannery, but you're also looking at the latest inspiration in paper arts. Leather and suede aren't just for your lived-in couches or for your favorite jacket. They are fitting fabrics for book covers, page backgrounds or accents. Harness a few new techniques from these projects and you'll be rounding up compliments from your friends and family.

THE TANNERY JOURNAL
BY JULIE V.

Cover book with bookbinder's cloth. Cover chipboard with leather. Embellish with ruler, belt and letters mounted on leather. Use leather stamps to stamp title into leather. Affix embellished leather to front of journal.

INTERTWINED
BY CAROL

Cut leather pieces to fit the front and back of journal and set eyelets on spine side. Transfer an image to Lazertran. Place decal in water, then adhere to leather with glue. Lay paper towels over area and brayer in place. When dry, age with shoe polish. Glue leather to the covers, adding waxed linen through the eyelets.

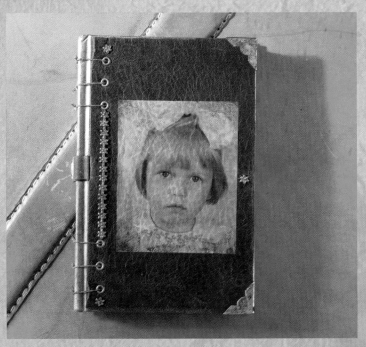

KAW-U-TZ
BY RUTH

Layer background with leather swatches. Stitch muslin to page, including leather lacing in the stitching. Sand metal, then place in bleach for two hours. Use to mat photo.

Kaw-u-tz (Cado)
Arkansas City,
Kansas 1906

IMAGE ON LEATHER
BY DONNA

Print a photo onto iron-on inkjet transfer paper, then iron it onto leather. Cut a rectangular hole in brown leather and back it with the transferred photo. Bind with lacing strips made by cutting leather in a spiral.

TRASH BAG
BY DONNA

At a photo-processing studio, have a photo applied to vinyl. Cut into a front and back piece, two sides and one bottom piece. Top stitch the pieces together to form a bag. Add handles and gold locks. Print words on a transparency, then use an iron-on transfer to affix it to the bag.

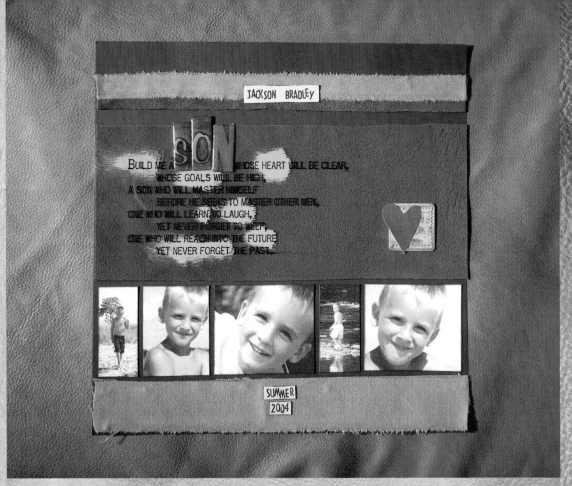

JACKSON BRADLEY

SON

BUILD ME A [SON] WHOSE HEART WILL BE CLEAR,
WHOSE GOALS WILL BE HIGH,
A SON WHO WILL MASTER HIMSELF
BEFORE HE SEEKS TO MASTER OTHER MEN,
ONE WHO WILL LEARN TO LAUGH,
YET NEVER FORGET TO WEEP,
ONE WHO WILL REACH INTO THE FUTURE
YET NEVER FORGET THE PAST.

SUMMER 2004

BUILD ME A SON
BY CATHY

Cut suede and leather into strips and add to background. Print photos in sepia tone. Print journaling on a transparency and paint the back of the transparency to highlight key words.

UTAH PONY
BY ANN

Collage fabric pieces and machine stitch to background. Add a photo printed on canvas. Attach cording with couching stitch and fray loose ends.

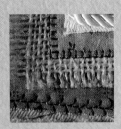

Utah

FRAMED FABRIC BOOK
BY JULIE V.

Stitch twill to book-binder's fabric. Cover three pieces of chipboard (a front and back cover and a spine) with the fabric to make book cover. Glue the back cover of a spiral journal inside the back cover. Embellish small frames and adhere to cover.

WISDOM
BY TENA

Draw a pattern onto cardstock, then cut it into three pieces. Using the pattern, cut three different faux leather pieces and adhere to background cardstock. Machine stitch 1/8" from all the edges. Hammer gold nailheads through the top and bottom edges.

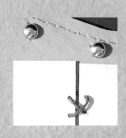

CHAPTER 8

Tailor

If you're searching for ways to alter a project, make a stop at the Tailor's. This store is full of high-fashion ideas to add texture and richness to projects that require a more masculine touch. Jennifer nipped a piece from a dress shirt and tie and tucked it on a layout while Julie used flat-felled seams to inspire her work. When you use fabrics or stitching characteristic of a tailor, you add instant class to your creations.

WORLD WAR II BY DONNA

Assemble various pieces of memorabilia in a shadow box, including fabric from a uniform.

THE LITTLE GENTLEMAN
BY RUTH

Dye one swatch of wool with green dye. Add decorative machine stitching around the edge of each swatch. Attach labels, buttons and watchfaces.

MY GUYS
BY JENNIFER

Cut sleeve from men's shirt and cut the end off a tie. Patch together with other fabrics to create background. Stamp on the fabric with chalk ink. Print journaling on transparency.

My guys.

Dave – Our supportive friend, teaching us how to enjoy life.
Scott – My collage buddy who has made me smile more than anyone else.
Keith – My new brother-in-law who sings like an angel.
Ken – So proud to call him my husband. Love him madly.
Mike – The best brother in the whole world. No arguing that.
Chris – No one brings on instant laughter like him.
Troy – Young and brilliant. Nothing is more important than family.
Marshall – The perfect example of how to take life less seriously and enjoy it more.
Matt – My best friend through the years.

Love these guys.

GRANDFATHER
BY DONNA

Stitch photo directly on cardstock and embellish with old suiting fabric and buttons.

Roland Augustus Fredrick TREDREA
GRANDFATHER (MIDDLE) 1946.

"My BABy"

Feeling left out that Jackson & Ellie

look just like me - Daddy has called you "My baby"

since the first minute of your life

Summer 2004

MY BABY
BY CATHY

Make fabric flowers by cutting petals out of various cotton, wool felt and tweed fabrics. Attach with glue dots and place button in center.

Graduate

determined

Excellence

so PROUD

A famous poet said, "Education is not the filling of a bucket but the lighting of a fire." John, as you graduate from eighth grade and move on to high school, may your fire burn brightly. — SUMMER 2004

CONFIDENCE

THE GRADUATE
BY JULIE T.

Sew three pieces of wool fabric together using flat-felled seams (see detailed directions on page 68). Tuck labels, journaling and photos under the seams before the final stitching. To create the left and right edges of the layout, fold the fabric under and press.

CO

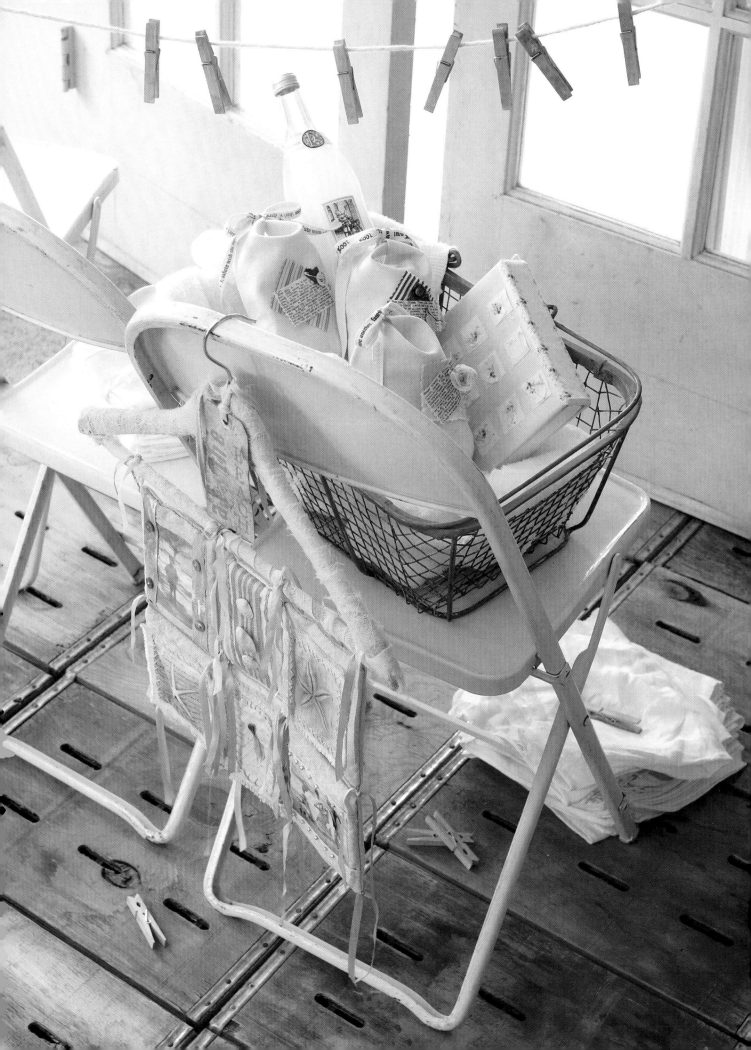

Laundry

Laundry changed dramatically with the invention of the electric washer in 1908, and it's being wrung through the wringer again as inspiration for scrapbooking. Julie purposely shrinks ribbon for a delicate touch on her *Young Lady* page while Debbie let laundry bags inspire the closure on her project. Washed, faded fabrics give a soft, comfortable feel to book covers, wall hangings and page layouts. Forget the detergent and the dryer sheets as you bring a fresh air to your projects with these all-new laundry techniques.

LAUNDRY BAGS
BY DEBBIE

Cut canvas to 8 1/2" x 10" inches. Turn under long edge and stitch. With right sides together, stitch along short edges making a tube. Put the seam in back and stitch across bottom of bag. Add eyelets at the top, and pin a sentiment to bag. Tie closed with ribbon.

SHABBY BOOK
BY DONNA

Cover a book with homemade book cloth (see page 68). Decorate with little squares of cotton fabric.

AT THE BEACH
BY CAROL

Scan and print images onto fabric. Attach images to squares and embellish. Attach ribbon to each corner and pillow sew the fronts onto a coordinating fabric. Turn right side out, hand stitch closed and tie the squares together. Cover a wooden hanger with gauzy fabric and tie squares to hanger.

GLIMPSES
BY CATHY

Collage the background with fabric swatches. Add photos and a title.

OCEAN TREASURE
BY TENA

Hand stitch accents and a title onto fabric. Mat the photo with a basket weave fabric and frame with seam tape. Stamp journaling on seam tape and stitch to the layout.

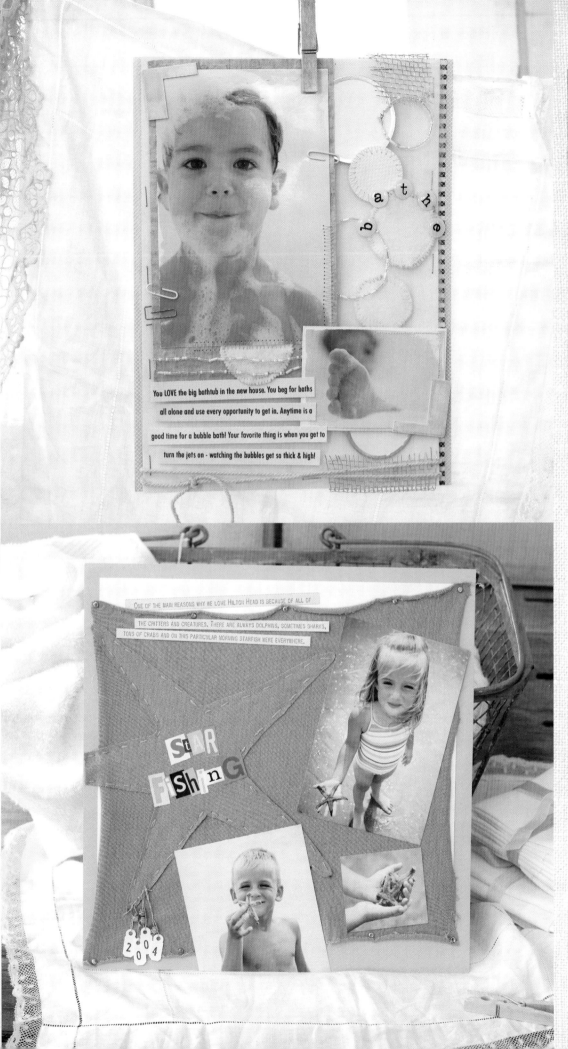

You LOVE the big bathtub in the new house. You beg for baths all alone and use every opportunity to get in. Anytime is a good time for a bubble bath! Your favorite thing is when you get to turn the jets on - watching the bubbles get so thick & high!

ONE OF THE MAIN REASONS WHY WE LOVE HILTON HEAD IS BECAUSE OF ALL OF THE CRITTERS AND CREATURES. THERE ARE ALWAYS DOLPHINS, SOMETIMES SHARKS, TONS OF CRABS AND ON THIS PARTICULAR MORNING STARFISH WERE EVERYWHERE.

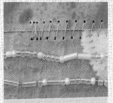

BATHE
BY LESLIE

Form beaded wire into circles. Adhere tulle to blue cardstock, then add a strip of patterned paper on the right-hand side. Wrap white cardstock with cream tulle and adhere in place. Sand the edges of the photos, then mat and affix to layout. Cut a slide holder to create photo corners. Stitch the edges of felt and cardstock circles.

STAR FISHING
BY CATHY

Rip up an old t-shirt to make the background. Sketch a starfish on the t-shirt and cut out. Add to background for a tone-on-tone effect.

JILLIAN

ADVICE TO A YOUNG LADY
BY JULIE T.

Shrink ribbon according to the directions on page 68. Tuck mini journaling strips into ribbon loops.

HANDS
BY RUTH

Paint frame with acrylic paint. Machine stitch fabric pieces on top of batting. Add hand stitching along with pearls and antique buttons.

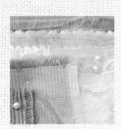

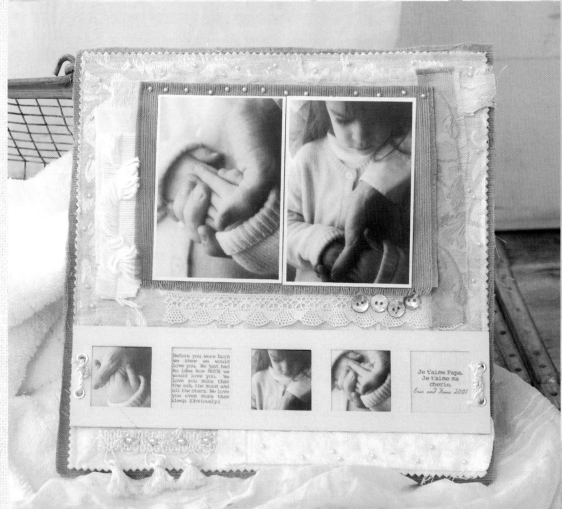

SWEET GRANDMA
BY JENNIFER

Stitch various sheers and lace over card-stock rectangles. Add pins and ribbons and stitch the journaling strips in place.

The journaling on the photo reads:
..the
sweetest
face in all
the world,
..my sweet grandma.

EM'S BRIDAL CLOSET
BY ANN

Decoupage the top layer of a floral napkin to vinyl fabric. When thoroughly dry, embellish cover, then line with fabric. Set large grommets and bind with ribbon, including filler paper in the binding.

ARTIST TIPS: Napkins or tissue paper work best for this technique as heavier paper is too thick and peels off.

Pharmacy

Need a quick remedy for your ailing pages? Come to the Pharmacy for a concoction of cool ideas. Learn the basics of batiking and become an expert on dying fabric with everything from tea and coffee to Kool-Aid and bleach. And before you leave, check out how Ann doctored up her travel art kit with custom twill labels. Take a lesson from the pharmacist as you formulate tonics to add life to your projects.

ALTERED FABRICS
BY RUTH

Tear squares of tea-dyed fabric and stitch in a random patchwork with wrong sides together. Snip from the torn edge to just before the seam. Rub the seams until they fray. Affix to the book cover. Put tags in a small Ziploc, adding three to six droppers-full of dye and rubbing it over the tags.

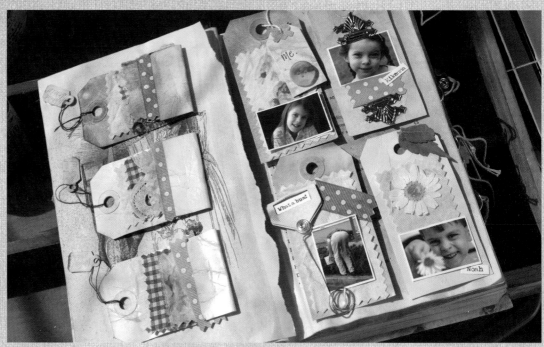

FLOWERS FOR MAMA
BY RUTH

Dye fabric, ribbon and tags with Kool-Aid, tea and coffee. For the Kool-Aid dye, mix Kool-Aid, one cup of hot water and one teaspoon salt. Adhere textured fabric to book board, then add layered tea-dyed fabric. Print journaling on silk ribbon.

LIVE, LAUGH, LOVE
BY RENEE

Stitch walnut-inked tags to background. Using bleach as the ink, stamp images onto tags. Paint edge of layout with bleach. Paint colorwash ink onto stamp image and press onto cream fabric. Use bleach on additional fabrics to create washed-out effect. Print journaling onto fabric piece, then stitch to page. Write words with a calligraphy pen dipped into bleach solution.

EYES
BY JENNIFER

Paint foam stamp with bleach and stamp directly onto fabric. When completely dry, color in with colored pencils or pastels. Assemble, leaving one piece of fabric loose to hide journaling.

NOT SO SWEET
BY TRACY

Using various widths of masking tape, tape off sections of fabric. Mix a concentrated solution of Kool-Aid and put in spray bottle. Spray lightly over fabric, let dry and remove masking tape. Stitch fabric to cardstock. Add torn strips of fabric. Tie fabric on stencil and add t-pin with a bead for accent.

GIFT BAG AND JOURNAL
BY CAROL

Paint a muslin bag with acrylic. Iron on postcards and add a coordinating fabric. Paint entire bag with tea-dye varnish. When dry, apply a base coat of crackle medium and dry. Apply a top coat of crackle and allow to dry. Antique with shoe polish or antiquing medium. For the journal, glue postcard paper on cover. When dry, age by following the same steps as the bag. Brush varnish on the enamel plate, then add to the cover.

HAVE JOURNAL, WILL TRAVEL
BY ANN

Lay out supplies to determine kit size and placement in kit. Print twill labels and stitch in place. Sew "pockets" on the canvas to accommodate supplies, allowing extra fabric for the depth of the items. Sew flaps to cover supplies and attach ties to hold flaps down. Stitch printed quotations to the cover. Sew handles to the outside cover fabric. To line, stitch cover piece to pocket piece with right sides together, leaving a 5" opening to turn. Turn inside out and stitch opening closed.

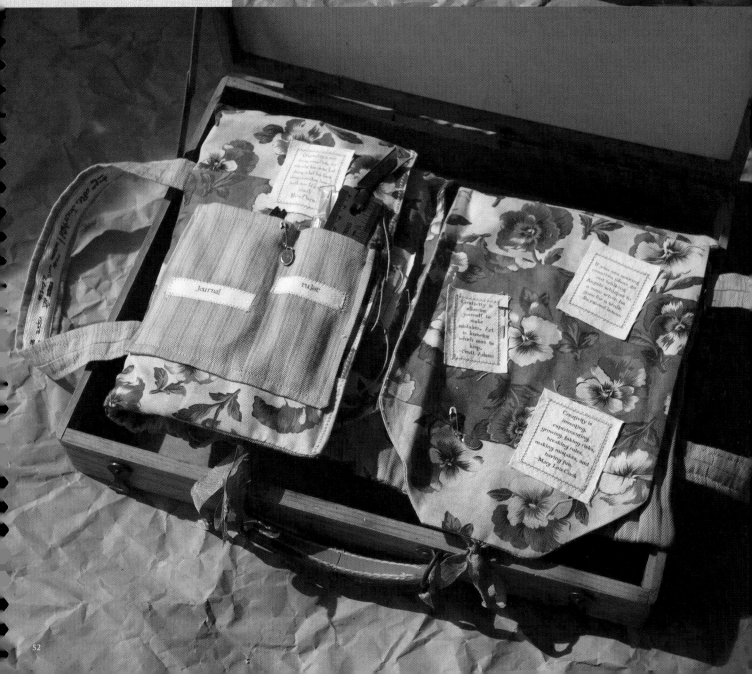

Creativity is inventing, experimenting, growing, taking risks, breaking rules, making mistakes, and having fun.
—Mary Lou Cook

SUMMER BEAUTY
BY TENA

Sketch a design onto cotton fabric. Apply melted paraffin wax over design and on a lettering template to make the title. Prepare a dye bath according to manufacturer's directions. Brush dye on the fabric and over the wax. When dry, sandwich the fabric between newspaper and iron on medium heat to remove the wax. Wash the fabric in warm water with a gentle soap to further remove excess wax and residue. Hang to dry. Iron on photos to the dried fabric and sand the edges of the photos. Adhere fabric to chipboard and stamp journaling onto twill.

COMMON THREADS
BY RENEE

Overlay lettering template onto swatch of fabric. Completely wipe over entire template with VersaMark ink. Heat emboss letters with clear embossing powder. Brush over embossed letters with color wash inks. Sew fabric to background.

54

At 13, Jordan stands on the edge of the ocean and the edge of womanhood. We are so proud of the young woman she is becoming.

hawaii

may

2003

JORDAN AT 13 BY JULIE T.

To dye lace and cotton velveteen, mix three colors of dye. Pre-wet the lace and velvet before dying to help the color take more evenly. Lay the velvet on a flat, protected surface and randomly spoon the different colors of dye over the fabric to create a mottled color effect. When done, rinse the fabric and hang to dry. Randomly dip the lace in the different colors. Rinse or blot off excess dye with a paper towel and hang to dry.

Gallery

CHAPTER 11

Follow our artists through the halls of this most creative Gallery. Reflect on this grouping of fabulous ways to frame photos or journaling. Take away ideas for your own home gallery by exploring Donna's ingenious use of a plain, stretched canvas or Tena's layout bursting with irresistible ideas for displaying photos and text. Grab your notebook, make a few sketches and enjoy the tour.

PILLOW TALK
BY DEBBIE

Sew fabric (right sides together) on three sides, stuff, turn right side out and hand stitch the fourth side closed. Decorate the top of corsage pins with printed fabric, mini fabric squares and beads. Stack small fabric squares at the bottom and stitch with gold cord. Sew a ring in back to hang, and use as a memo board.

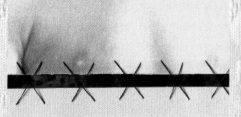

CONNOR CANVAS
BY DONNA

Cut out the center of a stretched canvas. Copy a photo onto printable fabric, then adhere the photo to the cut-out piece of canvas. Attach the canvas photo to the frame by first attaching the corners to get it even. Stitch to frame with large "X" stitches.

FRAME
BY DONNA

Cover a pre-purchased frame with fabric and ribbon. Adorn with a large button and photo turns.

SOUNDS FROM SARAH
BY DONNA

Transfer a photo onto fabric. Layer and sew pieces of fabric around the image to make a 12" x 12" scrapbook page. Print text on lightweight fabric and use to cover a button. Customize a vintage pin with rub-ons.

DRAWER KNOB BOOK
BY DONNA

Cover a blank book with patterned papers and ribbon. Secure a drawer knob to the front cover and a ribbon to the back cover to act as a 3-D closure.

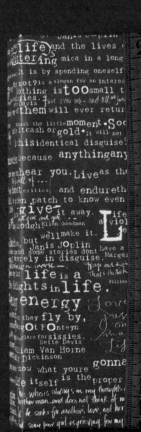

Having a sister is like a best friend you can't get rid of. You know whatever you do, they'll still be there. —Amy Li

Jones girls

lexa & britt

J

JONES GIRLS
BY TENA

Cover background with fabric and use ribbon, clips and easel spirales to attach photos to the layout. Cover buttons to match the ribbon.

MY LITTLE GALLERY
BY RUTH

Adhere velvet tapestry fabric to book board. Sand edges to age. Paint flower on sanded velvet with dimensional paint. Paint another flower on canvas. Glue two identical frames together with a photo or journaling in between.

My little Gallery

Haberdashery

Buttons, ribbon, tracing wheels and patterns: notions of all kinds are alive at the Haberdashery. Who knew the tools used with fabric could be an irresistible touch on a project? The inspiration provided by Tena's battalion of buttons and Jennifer's rows of rick rack just can't be measured. Let the artists fire your imagination and help bring more zip to your projects.

MADE IN THE SHADE
BY DEBBIE

Sew a basting stitch down the middle of each ribbon. Pull thread on one end to gather the ribbon, then knot the thread to keep it in place. Tuck the ends under and tack each ribbon to the lampshade. Glue on beaded fringe and tie a bow around the neck of the lamp.

MISSING YOU
BY DEBBIE

Stitch a scrap of fabric to the front of a card. Add a vintage button card, making sure one button is missing. Create custom envelopes from fabric and printed paper.

CONTRASTS

BY JULIE T.

Cut 16 3" squares of canvas. Mask off shapes on several of the squares. Dip each square into dye. Draw patterns onto the fabric squares with a sewing tracing wheel, colored transfer paper and a ruler. Dye a metal-rimmed tag and use to hold the large photo in place.

Before you were conceived

I wanted you

Before you

100%

contrasts

AGE TWELVE is a time of many moods, many changes, when everything is the same and everything is different. JACKSON seems to be navigating his way through these pre-teen years just fine and will meet his next big challenge when he begins junior high this fall.

GRACIE
BY DONNA

Cover the inside and outside of an accordion book with printed tissue, then stitch around the outside. Embellish with assorted notions. On the cover, attach fabric bits with a vintage pin and tie with ribbon. Print journaling on fabric, then stitch in place.

FINALLY
BY RUTH

Attach torn squares of fabric by tying a knot in the center of each with ribbon. Tie ribbon to large skirt pin and stitch to page.

MAEGAN
BY JENNIFER

Cover cardstock with adhesive. Line up rick rack to cover entire background. Allow the ends to hang off one end. Create journaling around photo.

were a little baby that fit perfectly in my arms. And now you are so big and becoming independent. But thankfully you still fit perfectly in my arms. XOXO. Your 2nd birthday. I can't believe it. You look so grown up. It seems like just yesterday you

maegan

LOVE YOU
BY MIRIAM

Stitch strips of ribbon to background and stitch rim of matted photo. Make sheer bags from two pieces of French ribbon and construct an envelope from muslin.

carlsbad

Maddie

Kenzie

Kristen

chErish your memories & rEmember

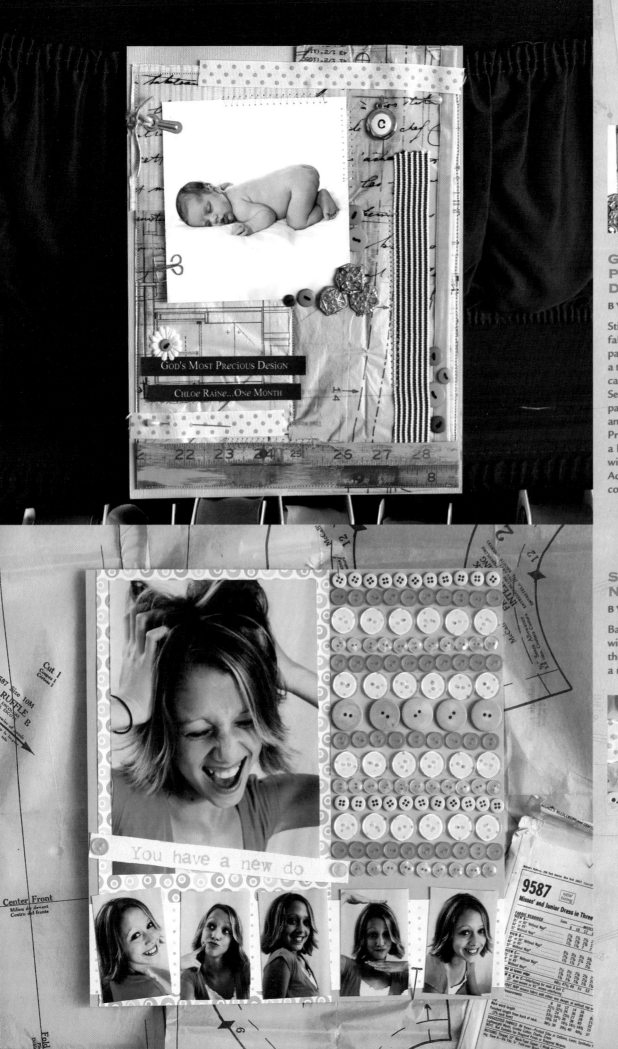

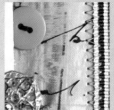

GOD'S MOST PRECIOUS DESIGN
BY LESLIE

Stitch tissue paper, fabric, ribbon, patterned paper and a transparency to a cardstock base. Secure photo with a paper clip, photo turn and sporadic stitches. Print journaling in a black text box with white text. Add buttons and corsage pins.

SHE'S GOT A NEW HAIR-DO
BY TENA

Back clear buttons with patterned paper, then affix to layout in a mosaic-like pattern.

THE Artists

Debbie Crouse

DEBBIE IS LIKE **SPANDEX**: HARDWORKING, RESILIENT AND SUPPORTIVE.

Donna Smylie

DONNA'S FABRIC OF CHOICE IS **VELCRO**. JUST LIKE HER, IT'S TENACIOUS, RELIABLE AND PRACTICAL.

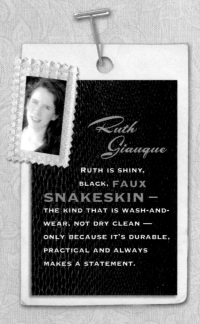

Ruth Giauque

RUTH IS SHINY, BLACK, **FAUX SNAKESKIN** — THE KIND THAT IS WASH-AND-WEAR, NOT DRY CLEAN — ONLY BECAUSE IT'S DURABLE, PRACTICAL AND ALWAYS MAKES A STATEMENT.

Carol Wingert

THE FABRIC THAT BEST DESCRIBES CAROL IS **LINEN** BECAUSE IT'S DURABLE, TIMELESS, CASUAL AND AGES WELL (IN FACT, IMPROVES WITH AGE!).

Tena Sprenger

OXFORD CLOTH COTTON, LIKE TENA, IS CASUAL BUT FANCY, DURABLE BUT STILL COMFORTABLE AND EASY TO WEAR. AND MOST IMPORTANTLY, IT DOESN'T LOOK TOO BAD WITH A FEW WRINKLES!

Julie Turner

CASHMERE RESEMBLES JULIE. BOTH ARE TIMELESS, WARM AND ALWAYS THERE FOR YOU.

Cathy Blackstone

WHITE, WRINKLE-FREE **OXFORD** IS CATHY'S TRADEMARK FABRIC. IT MATCHES EVERYTHING, DOESN'T NEED TO BE IRONED, IS ROOMY, AND IS PLAIN AND SIMPLE JUST LIKE HER.

Reneé Camacho

RENEÉ IS LIKE **GINGHAM.** SHE IS LIKE THIS TIMELESS FABRIC WITH FLEXIBLE PROPERTIES IN THAT BOTH ARE ABLE TO BLEND AND TAKE ON THE NATURE OF THE PATTERNS AND PIECE IT IS PAIRED WITH.

Jennifer McGuire

JENNIFER FINDS HERSELF SIMILAR TO **VELVET:** WARM, COMFORTING AND HAPPIEST IN RED.

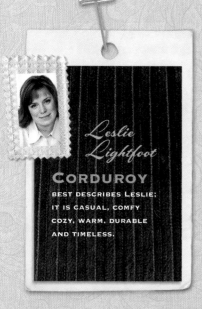

Leslie Lightfoot

CORDUROY BEST DESCRIBES LESLIE; IT IS CASUAL, COMFY COZY, WARM, DURABLE AND TIMELESS.

Julie van Oosten

JULIE CAN BE EASILY COMPARED TO **SILK** BECAUSE IT'S NATURAL AND COMES FROM HUMBLE BEGINNINGS. ITS ANCESTRY STARTED IN CHINA, AS DID JULIE'S. SILK IS ALSO EVER CHANGING FROM RAW TO FINE AND ADAPTS WELL IN ANY ENVIRONMENT.

Tracy Kyle

TRACY IDENTIFIES HERSELF WITH **FLANNEL.** WHY? BECAUSE LIKE FLANNEL, SHE IS LOW MAINTENANCE, OUTDOORSY, WARM AND FEELS MOST COMFORTABLE AT HOME IN HER PAJAMAS.

Miriam Hahn

MIRIAM FINDS HERSELF LIKE PINK AND WHITE **TICKING:** CRISP AND CLEAN, BRIGHT AND CHEERFUL, CLASSIC AND TRADITIONAL.

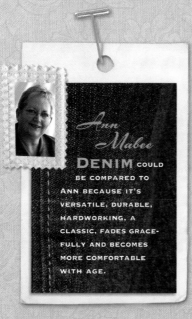

Ann Mabee

DENIM COULD BE COMPARED TO ANN BECAUSE IT'S VERSATILE, DURABLE, HARDWORKING, A CLASSIC, FADES GRACE-FULLY AND BECOMES MORE COMFORTABLE WITH AGE.

Janelle Smith

JANELLE IS LIKE DUPIONI **SILK.** IT IS LUSTROUS, OFTEN BRIGHTLY COLORED AND HAS WONDERFUL TEXTURE. THIS FABRIC ALSO DOESN'T WRINKLE EASILY OR HOLD A CREASE AND IS RELA-TIVELY EASY TO WORK WITH.

Materially
SPEAKING

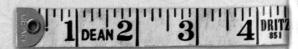

MAKING BOOK CLOTH

To make book cloth, iron fusible interfacing to the back of fabric. Remove the backing and iron mulberry paper over the interfacing.

SHRINKING RIBBON

Cut two pieces of water-soluble fabric about 25% larger than needed for the finished piece. Layer horizontal strips of ribbon onto one piece of the fabric, leaving a small space in between each ribbon. Then add a layer of vertical ribbons over the first layer. Leave a tiny space between each ribbon. (There is no need to weave the ribbon together because they will be stitched together.) Cover the ribbon with another layer of the fabric and pin the layers together to keep the ribbons from slipping out during sewing. Using Grilon shrinking thread on the bobbin and regular thread on top, stitch between each ribbon, both horizontally and vertically, making it look like a grid. Rinse the fabric in lukewarm water until all the soluble fabric is gone. Dip the ribbon fabric into very warm water according to the shrinking thread directions. The thread will shrink, causing the ribbon to gather up.

FLAT-FELLED SEAMS

With the wrong sides of the fabric together, stitch a plain seam. Open the fabric so the wrong sides are no longer together. Press the seam allowances to one side, so one seam allowance lays on top of the other. Trim the underneath seam allowance to 1/8". Turn under 1/4" of the top seam allowance and baste it in place over the trimmed edge. (For quick sewing, use pins or glue stick instead of hand basting.) Edgestitch close to the fold. (taken from www.simplicity.com)

TURNING FABRIC INTO PAPER

To turn a favorite fabric into a piece of paper, scan a piece of the fabric, then print it on cardstock. Or with a color copier/printer/scanner combo, simply lay the fabric on the scanner bed and make a color copy onto cardstock.

PRINTING TEXT ON FABRIC

To print on fabric, print text onto paper. Cover the text with double-sided tape, then secure the fabric over the top. Send through the printer again. To print on an entire piece of fabric, affix fabric to a carrier, such as freezer paper, then run through the printer.

PRINTING PHOTOS ON FABRIC

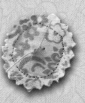

Scan a photo or download one from a digital camera. Cut fabric to 8 1/2" x 11", then adhere it to a carrier such as freezer paper or fusible interfacing. Print the photo, printing on the fabric instead of paper.

TIPS FOR DYING FABRIC

Natural fabrics take dye better and dye more vividly than synthetic fabrics. Wetting the fabric before dying helps it dye more evenly. Use the hottest water possible to obtain deeper colors and to dye the fabric faster. When using Rit or Kool-Aid, use a vinegar rinse after dyeing to help "set" the color.

FABRIC USED ON OUSIDE
AND INSIDE COVERS BY ART
OF THE MIDWEST COPYRIGHT
BY AMY BUTLER

CHAPTER 1

Paperie

Pages 4-9

THE BRIDE'S CLOSET
RIBBON: 7gypsies

WEDDING GIFT BOX
PAPER: Anna Griffin
and MM
RIBBON, TAGS, LABELS
AND SPIRALS: 7gypsies
LABELS AND SILK
FLOWERS: MM
BOX: Organized Living
TINS: Memory Lane

BRIGHT EYES
PAPER: Anna Griffin
FONT: Souvenir Light
KEYHOLE: 7gypsies

ALYSSA NICOLE
FABRIC: Moda Fabrics
RIBBON: Kobuko
TWINE: Memory Lane
RUB-ONS: MM

LEXI
FABRIC: Moda Fabrics
RIBBON: May Arts
RUBBER STAMPS: Alphabet
Stamps and Club Scrap
FABRIC STIFFENER:
Stiffy, Plaid

FEMININE
PAPER: Anna Griffin
METAL PLATE: Memory Lane
METAL CORNERS: 7gypsies
RIBBON: Bucilla
FLOWER: MM
FONT: BernhardMod,
WordPerfect

LOVE MANY THINGS
PAPER AND RUB-ON: AL
KEYHOLE: 7gypsies
RUBBER STAMP: Wordsworth

MIRACLE
STAMPS: MM
COLORWASH: 7gypsies
HINGES:
Karen Foster Design
PRINTABLE FABRIC:
Jacquard Products

GRANDMA'S JOURNAL
RIBBON: Ink It!
METAL ACCENT:
Karen Foster Design
BUTTONS: Dritz
WAXED LINEN: 7gypsies

CHAPTER 2

Bindery

Pages 10-13

HEART AND SOUL
BRASS STUDS AND CLOCK:
7gypsies
SILK FLOWERS, RIBBON AND
SAFETY PINS: MM

MATERIALLY SPEAKING
FABRIC: Ralph Lauren
BUTTONS: Mill Hill
BAMBOO CLIP: 7gypsies

PUPPY LOVE
RIBBON AND TWILL:
Memory Lane
FABRIC: Zoe's Trunk
BUTTONS AND PETITE TABS:
7gypsies
TYPEWRITER KEYS:
Westrim Crafts
SATIN ROSE AND SILK
LEAVES: Flights of Fancy
Boutique
FRAME: MM

I LOVE THEE
STAMPS: Hero Arts
PETITE TABS, CAMEO PIN,
TWILL, WAXED LINEN, TAG
AND GOLD CORNER: 7gypsies

SKETCH JOURNAL
SKETCH BOOK, TWILL, RIB-
BON AND BUTTONS: 7gypsies

NON-NAKED JOURNALS
FABRIC: Ralph Lauren
TWILL AND TAG BOOK:
7gypsies

CHAPTER 3

Boutique

Pages 14-17

SILK FABRIC JOURNAL
STAMPS: Collections
RIBBON, TWILL AND STRING:
The Thread Studio

CORSET BOOK
"D" RINGS:
Li'l Davis Designs
GOLD LOCKET: Anima Designs
CAMEO: Flights of Fancy
Boutique

FABRIC GIFT BOX
FRAMES AND LETTERS:
Collections

HANA MY GEM
JEWELRY TAG: 7gypsies
FONT: Handcrafted, AL

HORTON PLAZA
FABRIC PAPER: K & Co.
FONT: CK Stylish Black
GROMMETS: Dritz
BEAD CHAIN: Boxer
Scrapbook Productions

THE WORLD IS YOUR CANVAS
RUB-ONS: CI and Li'l
Davis Designs

JOYFUL SOUL
PAPER: K & Co.
FABRIC: MAMBI and
K & Co.
DEFINITION: FoofaLa
TYPEWRITER LETTERS: CI
BUTTERFLY ACCENT: Boxer
Scrapbook Productions
NETTING: Magic Scraps
RIBBON: Scrapbook
Wizard and MM

CHAPTER 4

Lingerie

Pages 18-21

EMALI'S TURN
GLASS FRAME:
Pottery Barn

EM'S A BRIDE
RIBBON, SPIRAL PIN, BEAD
AND BUTTONS: 7gypsies

FOR ME?
RIBBON AND COLORWASH:
7gypsies

ALL DOLLED UP
PAPER: Pulsar and
Artistic Scrapper
FONT: Old Remington, AL

SASSY AUDREY
FONT: Handcrafted, AL; 2Peas
Fancy Free
PAPER: K & Co.
STAMPS: Hero Arts
HOOKS: Dritz
MESH EYELETS: MM

BALLERINA
TINKER PINS: 7gypsies
RIBBON: Bucilla
FONT: Bernhard Modern,
WordPerfect

GRANDMA'S TRUNK
PAPER, RIBBON, CLASP AND
CARD HOLDER: 7gypsies
KEYS: River City Rubber Works
CEILING TIN:
Artistic Expressions

CHAPTER 5

Seamstress

Pages 22-25

SHOE
SNAPS: Dritz
RUB-ONS: AL

SWEET SAMANTHA
FABRIC: Moda Fabrics, Cranston Fabrics and Marcus Brothers Textiles
RIBBON: Midori and May Arts
FONT: 2Peas Bleached Blonde
FROG CLOSURE: Coats and Clark
FIBERS: Timeless Touches
METAL LETTERS: MM

TEA
NAPKIN: Target
COASTERS: Marshalls
RIBBON: Memory Lane, Melrose Vintage and Girly Girlz
FABRIC LETTERS: Li'l Davis Designs
PAPER, TAGS, FRAME, SILVER RING, FRAME AND SILVER CLIP: 7gypsies

TRAITS
FONT: 2Peas Tasklist
PHOTOS: Tammy Batson

SUNSHINE
PAPER: AL, CI and KI Memories
TISSUE PAPER: 7gypsies
TRANSPARENCY: CI
FIBER: Scrapbook Wizard
FABRIC PAPER: MAMBI

UNQUESTIONABLY YOU
BUTTON: 7gypsies
PAPER: Chronicle Books

CHAPTER 6
Nursery
Pages 26-33

GRACIE'S DRESS
PAPER AND DOORKNOB: 7gypsies
FRAME: Eddie Bauer Home

THUMBS UP
DISHTOWEL: Marshalls
RIBBON: Memory Lane
STAMPS: MM and Ma Vinci's Reliquary
FONT: CK Typewriter
BOTTLE, CLOTHESPINS AND BUTTONS: 7gypsies
BRADWEAR DECALS: CI

CURTAIN CALL
RIBBON AND CLIPS: 7gypsies
CURTAIN RINGS AND ROD: Pottery Barn

LAYETTE
BUTTONS AND PAPER: 7gypsies
MUSLIN PAPER: Avery
BOOTIE PATTERN: Vogue

BABY OZZIE
INKJET FABRIC: Jacquard Products
RIBBON: May Arts and 7gypsies
COVERED-BUTTON KIT: Dritz
BOTTLE: 7gypsies

CUTER
RUB-ONS: AL
FONT: Capone, AL
CLAY CIRCLE: Li'l Davis Designs

WILL AGE 2
FABRIC: Harper Fabric
TWILL: May Arts
STAMPS: Image Tree
BOOK PLATE: Li'l Davis Designs
"BOY" LABEL: Junkitz
LETTERING TEMPLATE: Scrap Pagerz

K
CANVAS PAPER: MAMBI
TRANSPARENCY NEGATIVE: CI
HEMP FABRIC: Artistic Scrapper
WORD ACCENTS: KI Memories
LEATHER ACCENTS: MM
LONG BARS: 7gypsies
PAPER: Mustard Moon

POCKET BOOK
TAGS, STICKERS, WATCH CRYSTAL AND HEMP: 7gypsies
CARDBOARD LETTERS AND WOODEN FLOWER: Li'l Davis Designs
METAL TAG: Anima Designs
METAL LETTERS: MM

FOURTH OF JULY
FONT: Worn Machine, AL
STAMPS: Hero Arts and MM
LINEN THREAD: Hillcreek Designs

JOSHUA'S BEST STUFF
NAILHEADS: American Tag
TABS: 7gypsies
WAXED COTTON AND RIM: Memory Lane
PHOTO CANVAS: Avery
ESCUTCHEON: Ink It!
STAMPS: Postmodern Design, Stampers Anonymous and Hero Arts

CHAPTER 7
Tannery

Pages 34-37

THE TANNERY JOURNAL
JOURNAL EMBELLISHMENTS: Collections

INTERTWINED
KRAFT BOARD BOOK: Westrim Crafts
WAXED LINEN, BRASS FLOWERS AND CORNERS: 7gypsies
LETTER "I": K & Co.
IMAGE TRANSFER: Lazertran
GOLD LEAF PEN: Krylon

KAW-U-TZ
BEADS: Drumbeat Indian Arts
WAXED LINEN: 7gypsies

TRASH BAG
GOLD LOCKS: 7gypsies

BUILD ME A SON
STAMPS: Hero Arts
STICKERS: K & Co. and Pebbles
FONT: Old Remington, AL
TAG: MM

UTAH PONY
FABRIC: Cabbage Rose and Quilter's Bee
FONT: Texas Hero
LEATHER FLOWER: MM
BUTTONS: JHB International
CHARM PIN: Create-a-Craft
CHARMS, LEATHER AND CONCHO: Friendze
RICK RACK: Cabbage Rose
TWILL: SAS
CORDING: Wrights

FRAMED FABRIC BOOK
ANTIQUE RULERS AND JOURNAL EMBELLISHMENTS: Collections

WISDOM
STAMPS: Junque

CHAPTER 8
Tailor
Pages 38-41

WORLD WAR II
SHADOW BOX: Pottery Barn

THE LITTLE GENTLEMAN
GREEN DYE: Ranger Industries
WATCHFACES, TAGS AND BUCKLE: 7gypsies

MY GUYS
STAMPS: Impression Obsession
LETTER BRADS: Colorbök
PHOTO: Angela Talentino

MY BABY
RUB-ONS: Li'l Davis Designs
FONT: 2Peas Miss Happy
LINEN THREAD: Hillcreek Designs
DATE STAMP: MM

THE GRADUATE
CLOTH LABELS: MAMBI

CHAPTER 9
Laundry
Pages 42-47

LAUNDRY BAGS
TWILL, TAG AND SENTIMENTS: 7gypsies

SHABBY BOOK
FUSIBLE INTERFACING: Wonder Under

AT THE BEACH
RIBBON, TAG AND COLORWASH: 7gypsies
STAMPS: Postmodern Design and Hero Arts

GLIMPSES
FONT: Bauer Bodini
CHARM: Quest Beads
LINEN THREAD: Hillcreek Designs

OCEAN TREASURE
RIBBON: May Arts
FIBERS: Timeless Touches, On the Surface and MM
STAMPS: Image Tree
SEAM TAPE: Coats and Clark
LETTERING TEMPLATE: Wordsworth

BATHE
PAPER: Mustard Moon and Sanook
METAL MESH: MM
LETTER STICKERS: Li'l Davis Designs

STAR FISHING
STICKERS: MM
FONT: Old Remington, AL
STAMPS: Hero Arts
LINEN THREAD: Hillcreek Designs

ADVICE TO A YOUNG LADY
RIBBON: 7gypsies
GRILON SHRINKING THREAD AND ROMEO WATER-SOLUBLE FABRIC: MeinkeToy

HANDS
FRAME: Die Cuts with a View

SWEET GRANDMA
FONT: 2Peas Renaissance
FLOWERS, LACE, CHEESE CLOTH AND SHEER FABRIC: Hobby Lobby
PINS: MM

EM'S BRIDAL CLOSET
NAPKINS: Party City
NEUTRAL GINGHAM: 35th Ave. Sewing
RIBBON: May Arts, MM and 7gypsies
FONT: Kelly
RUB-ONS: MM
GROMMETS: Dritz
LETTER "E": Novtex Corp.
FRAME: Nunn Designs

CHAPTER 10
Pharmacy
Pages 48-55

ALTERED FABRICS
JEWELRY TAGS AND COLORWASH: 7gypsies

FLOWERS FOR MAMA
LABEL: 7gypsies
FABRIC DYE: Ranger Industries and Rit
FONT: AL

LIVE, LAUGH, LOVE
FONT: Capone, AL
COLORWASH: 7gypsies
STAMPS: Image Tree, Hero Arts and Wordsworth
BUTTONS: EK Success

EYES
FONT: Uncle Charles, AL
STAMPS: Hero Arts, Hobby Lobby and MM

NOT SO SWEET
BUTTONS: K & Co.
STENCIL, RUB-ON AND POG: AL
BEADS: Blue Moon

GIFT BAG AND JOURNAL
FABRIC GIFT BAG: Sumcards, Inc.
TEA-DYE VARNISH: Rubber Stampede
CRACKLE-MEDIUM: Duncan
JOURNAL: Letterbox
POSTCARD PAPER: Stampington & Co.
RIBBON: Memory Lane
TISSUE & ENAMEL PLATE: 7gypsies
FABRIC: Ink It!

HAVE JOURNAL, WILL TRAVEL
FABRIC: Moda Fabrics
TWILL, ELASTIC AND BUTTONS: 7gypsies
RIBBON: Memory Lane & SAS
FONT: Black Boys on Mopeds
SAFETY PINS: MM
CHARMS: Artisan Stamps

SUMMER BEAUTY
CHIPBOARD: Memory Lane
STAMPS: PSX Design
LETTERING STENCIL: Wordsworth
FABRIC DYE: Rit
TRANSFER PAPER: Avery
PHOTOS: Dana Florence

COMMON THREADS
FONT: Handcrafted, AL
RIBBONS: EK Success and Offray
PAPER: Anna Griffin
LETTERING TEMPLATE: Wordsworth
BUTTON AND COLORWASH: 7gypsies
LEDGER TAB: AL

JORDAN AT 13
DYE AND TAGS: MM
RIBBON: Bucilla

CHAPTER 11
Gallery
Pages 56-59

CONNER CANVAS
PRINTABLE FABRIC: Hewlett Packard
TITLE PLATE: Memory Lane

PILLOW TALK
CORSAGE PINS: Fox
TASSELS: Wrights

SOUNDS FROM SARAH
SKIRT PIN AND DOOR KNOB: 7gypsies
RUB-ONS: AL

DRAWER KNOB BOOK
PAPER AND KNOB: 7gypsies

JONES GIRLS
RIBBON: May Arts and Midori
STAMPS: Postmodern Design and Stampers Anonymous
SPIRALES: 7gypsies
JUMP RINGS AND OVAL CLIPS: MM
SAFETY PIN: Li'l Davis Designs
COVERED-BUTTON KIT: Dritz
LETTER STICKER: Wordsworth
PHOTOS: Allison Tyler Jones

MY LITTLE GALLERY
FRAMES: Memory Lane
FONT: Masterpiece, AL

CHAPTER 12
Haberdashery
Pages 60-65

MADE IN THE SHADE
LAMP: Kirkland's

MISSING YOU
FABRIC: The Beginning Fabrics
MINI TAG: 7gypsies

CONTRASTS
TRACING WHEEL AND TRANSFER PAPER: Dritz
RIBBON: Mokuba
STICKERS, DYE AND TAG: MM

GRACIE
PAPER, TISSUE, ACCORDION BOOK, ELASTIC AND RIBBON: 7gypsies

FINALLY
RIBBON: MM
MINI BOOK: iota
GARTER: 7gypsies
STAMPS: PSX Design

MAEGAN
RICK RACK: Hap's Memories
FONT: 2Peas Fancy Free
ARCLYIC LETTERS: KI Memories
PHOTOS: Amy Grendell

LOVE YOU
RIBBON: 7gypsies and Memory Lane
TWILL: Memory Lane
FONT: CK Gutenburg and Bradley ITC
HOOKS AND EYES: Dritz
FRAME AND BOTTLE: 7gypsies
FABRIC WORDS: CI

GOD'S MOST PRECIOUS DESIGN
PAPER, TISSUE, TRANSPARENCY AND PHOTO TURN: 7gypsies
BUTTONS: MM
RIBBON: Scrapbook Wizard
CORSAGE PINS: Dritz
STICKER AND CHARM: Li'l Davis Designs
FONT: CK Chemistry

SHE'S GOT A NEW HAIR-DO
PAPER: SEI
PRINTABLE FABRIC: Memory Lane
FONT: Dislexiae
BUTTONS: SAS
RUB-ONS: AL

Designing With Fabric IS THE NEWEST ADDITION TO THE ESTEEMED Autumn Leaves DESIGNING WITH SERIES THAT INCLUDES THE FOLLOWING TITLES:

DESIGNING WITH VELLUM

DESIGNING WITH NOTIONS

DESIGNING WITH TEXTURE

DESIGNING WITH PHOTOS

DESIGNING WITH WORDS

DESIGNING WITH SIMPLICITY

FROM THE CATWALK TO YOUR CLOSET, FABRIC IS EVERYWHERE. AND NOW IT'S AN ESSENTIAL STAPLE FOR SCRAPBOOK PAGES, JOURNALS AND EVERY PROJECT IMAGINABLE. SAVOR YOUR COPY OF **DESIGNING WITH FABRIC** AND WATCH FOR MORE INNOVATIVE ADDITIONS TO OUR FLAGSHIP SERIES.